Warts

Michael P. Kinch

My Health

Franklin Watts

A Division of Grolier Publishing

New York • London • Hong Kong • Sydney

Danbury, Connecticut

For my two sweet warts, Ginger and Cindy

Photographs©: Corbis-Bettmann: 7; Custom Medical Stock Photo: 34 (S. Barao), 17 (Teri J. McDermott), 35 (Eric Nelson), 20, 33; Medical Images Inc.: 25 (Nancy Wolfin, M. D.); Monkmeyer Press: 39 (Heron); Peter Arnold Inc.: 6 bottom, 24 right (Zeva Delbaum), 4 (Marilyn Kazmers); Photo Researchers: 21, 29, 32 (Biophoto Associates), 8 (Ken Brate), 40 (Tim Davis), 10 left (A. B. Dowsett/SPL), 15 (David Gifford/SPL), 6 top, 30 (Dr. P. Marazzi/SPL), 26 (David Parker/SPL), 10 right (NIBSC/SPL), 11 (NCI/SPL), 13 (QUEST/SPL), 19 (Dr. Linda Stannard, UCT/SPL), 22 (John Watney/Science), 12 (Andrew G. Wood); Stock Boston: 27 (Frank Siteman); Visuals Unlimited: 24 left (Ken Greer), 37 (David M. Phillips).

Cartoons by Rick Stromoski

Visit Franklin Watts on the Internet at:
http://publishing.grolier.com

Library of Congress Cataloging-in-Publication Data

Kinch, Michael P.
    Warts / by Michael P. Kinch.
        p.   cm.—(My Health)
    Includes bibliographical references and index.
    Summary: Describes what a wart is, how to identify a wart, how warts spread, kinds of warts, and how to get rid of them.
    ISBN 0-531-11625-5 (lib. bdg.)   0-531-16453-5 (pbk.)
    1. Warts—Juvenile literature. [1. Warts] I. Title. II. Series.
RL471.K55   2000
616.5'44—dc21   98-53646
                                                                  CIP
                                                                  AC

ontents

What Is a Wart? **5**

What Causes a Wart? **8**

Your Amazing Skin. **13**

Three Kinds of Human Warts **20**

How Warts Spread. **27**

Getting Rid of Warts. **32**

Preventing Warts **37**

Glossary. **41**

Learning More **44**

Index **46**

What Is a Wart?

What do the Wicked Witch of the West, Keiko the killer whale, and a whole lot of humans have in common? You guessed it—**warts!** Warts are rough, tough, ugly bumps that suddenly appear on our skin. But they are more than just pesky skin lumps. They are amazingly complicated growths. Here's your chance to take a closer look at the mystery, the medicine, and the misery of warts.

How do you know if a bump on your skin is a wart? It's not always easy to tell. Some warts are a little lighter or a little darker than your skin, but most are about the same

Did You Know....

Toads and frogs can't give you warts! They may have bumpy skin, but those bumps aren't warts.

◀ **Keiko, the killer whale who starred in the movie *Free Willy*, now lives off the coast of Iceland. Would you believe Keiko has warts?**

5

color. When you touch a wart, it usually feels hard and tough. **Corns** on your foot can feel hard and tough too. But a wart's surface is different. It usually feels bumpy and may look like a tiny cauliflower. Sometimes

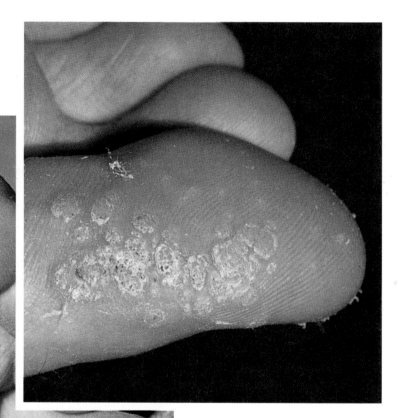

Corns (left) and warts (above) can look similar.

you can see dark specks inside a wart. If you have a bump that you think might be a wart, you should have a doctor look at it.

Fact or Fiction?

In the book *The Adventures of Huckleberry Finn* by Mark Twain, the main character claims that to get rid of a wart:

You got to go all by yourself, to the middle of the woods, where you know there's a spunk-water stump, and just as it's midnight you back up against the stump and jam your hand in and say, "Barley-corn, barley corn, injun meal shorts; Spunk-water, spunk-water, swaller these warts," and then walk away quick, eleven steps, with your eyes shut, and then turn around three times and walk home without speaking to anyone. Because if you speak the charm's busted.

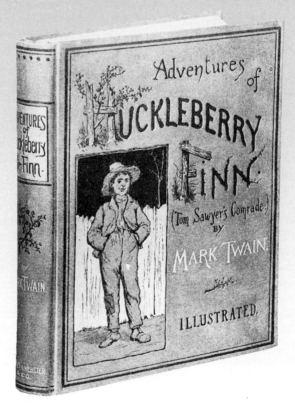

Mark Twain wrote *The Adventures of Huckleberry Finn* in 1885, but people still enjoy reading it.

What Causes a Wart?

To understand what a wart really is, imagine an anthill. An anthill doesn't just magically appear. It is built by thousands of ants. Inside the mound are dozens of tunnels and small rooms. This is where the ants rest, store food, and raise their young.

Would you believe that an anthill has something in common with a wart?

8

A wart is a like an anthill—it doesn't just grow by itself. A wart is created by germs called **viruses**. The viruses make the wart their home. It is where they make more viruses.

Viruses are tiny. They are so small that you can't even see them with a magnifying glass or a typical microscope. Scientists need powerful **electron microscopes** to see viruses.

The Romans Knew!

Virus is a word the ancient Romans used to mean "poison" or "slime." These tiny germs really can poison our cells.

Activity 1: How Small Is a Wart Virus!

It would take almost 3 million human wart viruses placed side by side to reach across the dot above the letter "i" on this page. Now that's small! If you want to figure out about how many wart viruses it would take to cover the entire surface of the dot above the "i," multiply 1,500,000 × 1,500,000 × 3. If so many wart viruses can fit in the dot on the letter "i," imagine how many can fit inside a wart!

There are thousands of kinds of viruses. Most can live in only one type of plant or animal. Some human viruses cause the common cold, while others cause chickenpox, polio, and the flu.

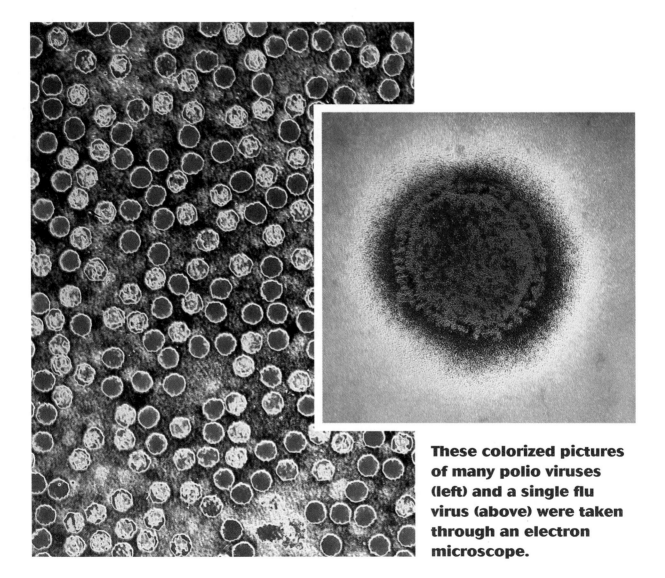

These colorized pictures of many polio viruses (left) and a single flu virus (above) were taken through an electron microscope.

The viruses that cause human warts are called **papilloma viruses.** Each papilloma virus has seventy-two sides and looks something like a tiny soccer ball. When a papilloma virus is outside of a living cell, it is **dormant.** A dormant virus is kind of like a shut-down computer—it doesn't do anything. A virus can't "switch on" unless it finds exactly the right kind of cells. Then it has to get inside those cells.

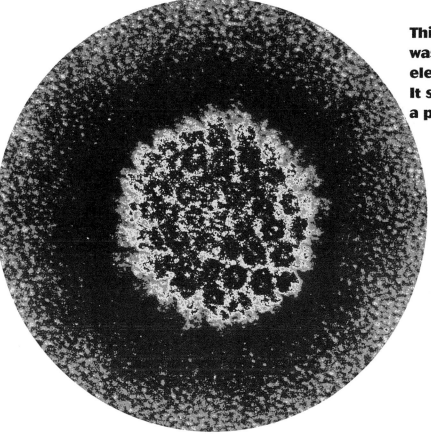

This colorized picture was taken through an electron microscope. It shows the shape of a papilloma virus.

A human papilloma virus can live inside human skin cells, but it cannot live in the skin cells of any other animal. It can't live in human liver cells either—or brain cells, muscle cells, or any other kind of cells. Since warts cannot live outside our skin, it is important to understand more about our wonderful skin.

A Warty World

Aren't you glad you can't get the same kind of warts as a green sea turtle?

Humans aren't the only animals that get warts. Chimpanzees, monkeys, cows, deer, dogs, horses, sheep, elephants, elk, opossums, mice, turtles, finches, parrots, whales, and manatees get them too.

You can't get the same kind of warts as a parrot or a whale, though. Each kind of animal gets warts from only one type of virus. Some viruses make only horse warts, and other viruses make only turtle warts. Dogs catch only dog wart viruses, and deer get only deer wart viruses.

Your Amazing Skin

Your skin covers your body and protects it from injury and disease. It keeps moisture in and germs, such as viruses and **bacteria,** out. Your skin is made up of billions of tiny cells.

The average skin cell lives 28 days. When it dies, new cells form and push the dead cells toward the

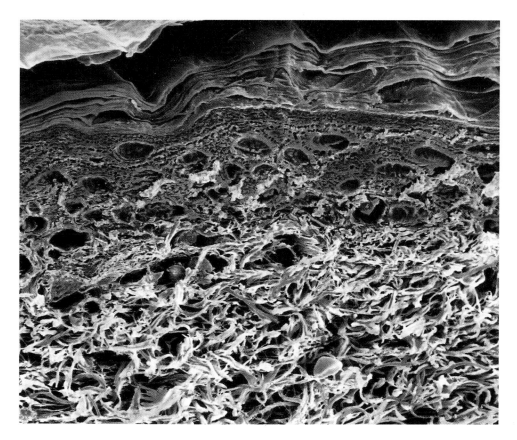

This is what your skin looks like through a powerful microscope. The colors have been added to make it easier to see where one layer stops and another starts.

surface of your skin. The dead cells squeeze together and flatten out to form a thick, tough outer layer of skin called the **keratin layer.**

The dead cells on the surface of your skin overlap like the shingles on a roof. Just as a roof keeps the rain out of your house, the keratin layer keeps most disease germs from getting through your skin. If the germs can't get in, they can't hurt you. The cells on your skin's surface also keep body fluids from leaking out.

Because the cells on the surface of your skin are dead, papilloma viruses can't use them to make more viruses. The viruses need to get down to the layers of living skin cells below the surface.

The top layer of living skin cells is called the **epidermis.** The layer below that is the **dermis.** The dermis makes up about 90 percent of your skin. The dermis has **glands** that give off sweat when you are hot and produce oils when your skin is dry. Your hair grows out of **hair follicles** in the dermis.

This drawing of the skin
shows a hair follicle, a sweat
gland, a nerve fiber network
(yellow), and blood vessels
(red and blue) running
through the skin and the
fatty layer beneath it.

The dermis also contains muscles and nerve endings. These nerves tell you when something is too hot or too cold. If you cut your finger, nerve endings in the dermis send messages to your brain that your finger is hurt.

The living cells in the dermis are nourished by millions of tiny blood vessels. The cells in the epidermis depend on the blood vessels in the dermis for the food and oxygen they need to live and grow.

Millions of viruses and other germs are on the surface of your skin right now. Some drifted through the air and landed on your skin. Others ended up on your skin when you touched some object. Most of these viruses just lie dormant on the surface of your skin. They can't do anything unless they get inside your body.

Your skin does a good job protecting you from outside invaders. But when you get a cut, dirt and germs can get inside your body. That can mean trouble. If a papilloma virus finds that cut, it can sneak into the epidermis and attach itself to a cell.

To get inside the cell, the virus plays a trick. The surface of every cell has many **receptors.** A cell receptor is like the lock on a door. It can only be opened with a key that fits it exactly. The outside of a

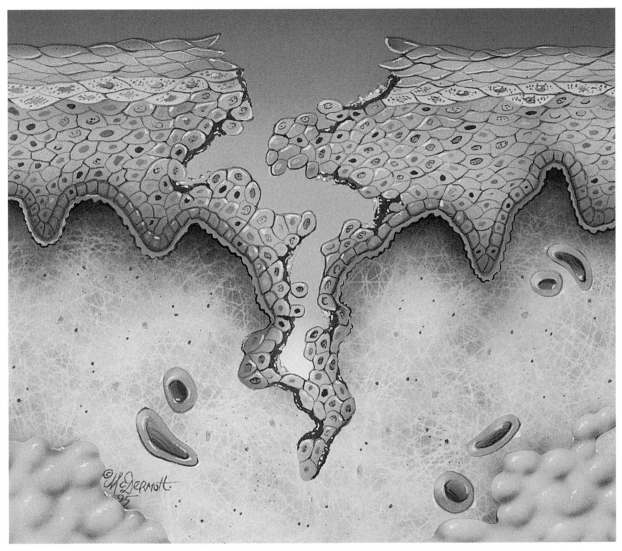

This drawing shows what happens when you get a cut.

papilloma virus has special **proteins** that fit the receptor perfectly. When the virus uses its "key," it can enter the skin cell.

Once the virus is inside, it turns the cell into a virus-making factory. It doesn't take long for one virus to produce thousands of new viruses. Many of the new papilloma viruses move to nearby skin cells and start their own virus factories. Soon the skin cells in the invaded area fill up with billions and billions of new viruses. Eventually, the skin cells are so full of viruses that they swell like tiny balloons. As the cells bulge in every direction, the epidermis pushes up against the top layer of skin. This little hill of virus-filled skin cells is the beginning of a wart.

Did You Know...

After a papilloma virus invades your skin, it takes between 1 and 6 months for a wart to develop.

JUNE

JAN FEB MAR APR MAY

This colorized picture ▶ of papilloma viruses was taken through an electron microscope.

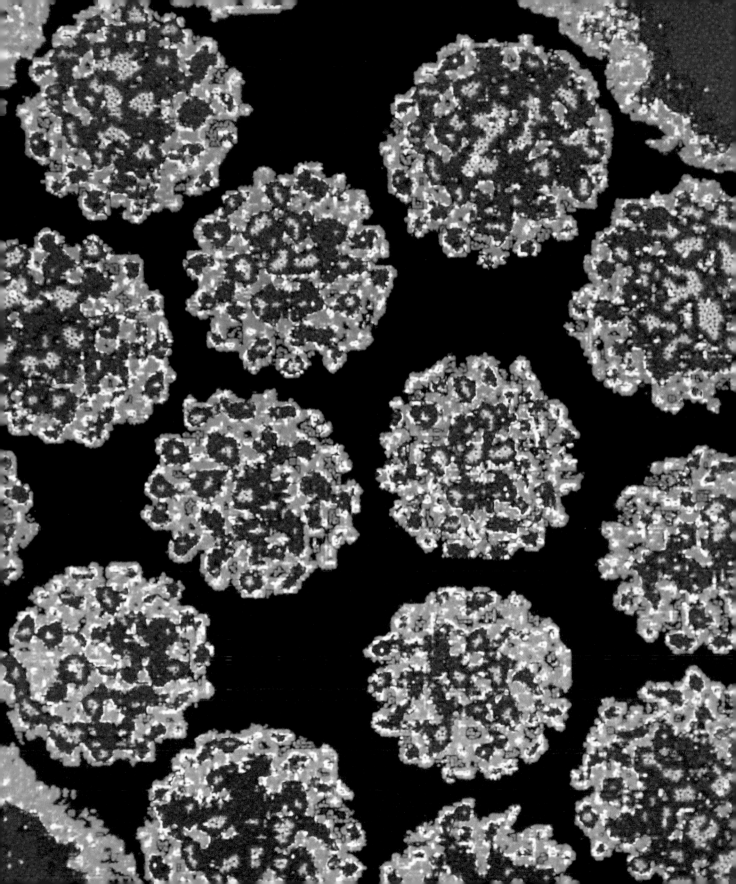

Three Kinds of Human Warts

There are many kinds of warts, but children usually get only three kinds. Most of the warts we see on people's hands and faces are called **common warts.** Common warts are usually about the size of a pea. They have a rough, bumpy surface and look a little like a cauliflower with dark specks.

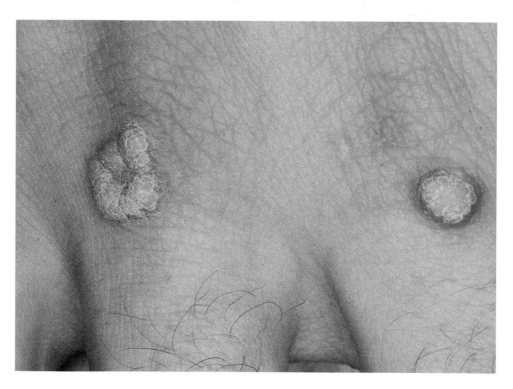

Common warts have a rough, bumpy surface.

Common warts look ugly, but they usually aren't painful.

Common warts usually grow on fingers, hands, and faces, but they can also spread to other parts of a person's body. Sometimes they itch, but they usually aren't painful—unless you snag one. Since warts stick up on your skin, you might accidentally catch one on clothing or another object. If you snag one hard enough, you could rip your skin. Ouch!

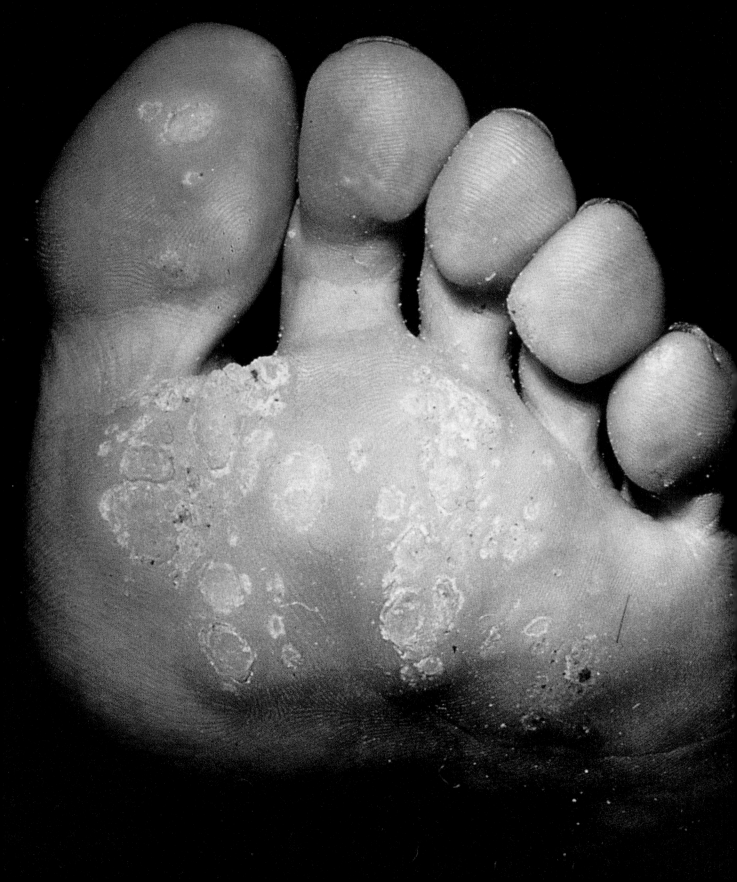

Warts that grow on the bottom of people's feet and toes are called **plantar warts.** The good news about plantar warts is that no one can see them if you keep your socks on. The bad news is that plantar warts can really hurt because the weight of your entire body presses down on them.

These warts try to grow out from the skin of your foot, but they can't because you're standing on them. The plantar warts end up pushing up into the tender flesh of your foot or toe instead.

Some plantar warts are tiny, but others grow as wide as a quarter. The bigger a plantar wart is, the deeper it grows, and the more it hurts. Sometimes these warts pop up in little groups called **colonies.**

◀ **A person with plantar warts may feel some pain when walking.**

Is It a Wart?

Sometimes it's hard to tell a plantar wart from a **callus.** And sometimes a callus forms around a plantar wart as your shoe rubs against your skin. If this happens, the callus gives the wart a waxy, yellowish look. But remember this:, If you can see little black dots, it's a wart.

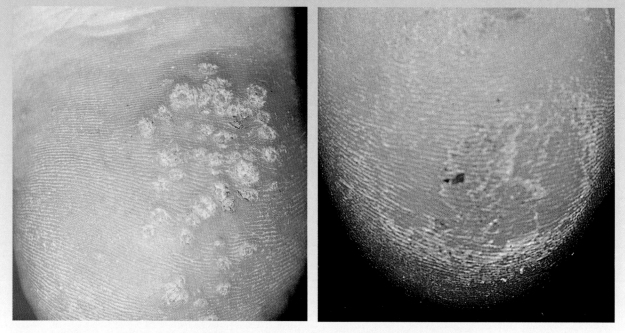

Sometimes plantar warts (left) can look like a callus (right).

What's the third type of wart? It's called a **flat wart.** Flat warts aren't completely flat, but they are smooth and don't stick up as much as common warts. Flat warts usually grow on a person's face, hands, arms, or legs.

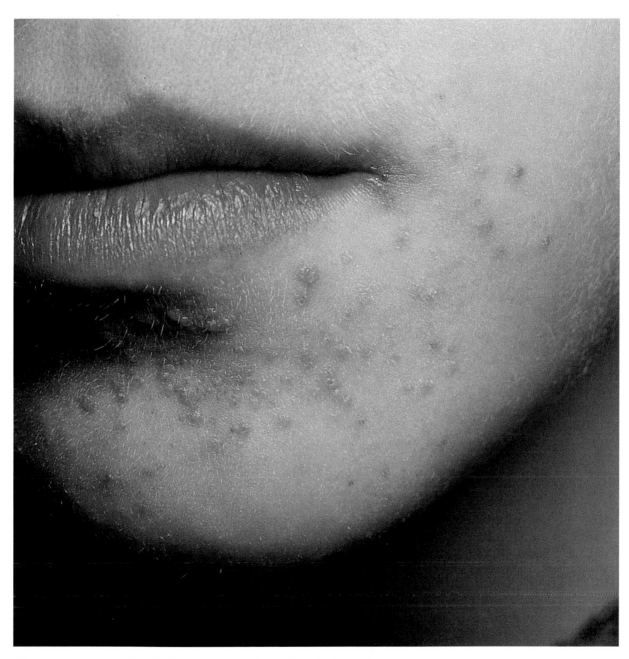

Flat warts can look like an outbreak of pimples.

The good news about flat warts is that they don't look too "warty." In fact, you may not even notice them at first. But the bad news is that flat warts usually come in groups. When people get flat warts, they get a lot of them—sometimes more than 100! They may look like an outbreak of pimples over areas of your skin.

Those Little Black Specks

The little specks in warts are the tops of small blood vessels called **capillaries.** These tiny blood vessels normally feed your cells, but warts use them to feed their growing wart factory. Because the capillaries look like tiny dots, some people call them "wart seeds." Others believe they are the tops of the wart's "roots." But a wart isn't a plant. It doesn't have roots, and it doesn't have seeds.

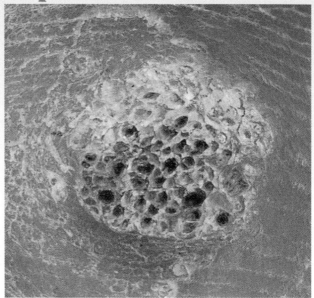

The black specks in this wart are capillaries.

How Warts Spread

Warts are **contagious.** That means you can get a wart by "catching" the papilloma virus.

Some people get warts more easily than others. Children seem to get the most warts. About 10 to 15 percent have warts. Are you one of them?

Even if you don't have warts, three or four people in your class at school probably do. That means you may catch warts from them. Almost everyone has warts at some time in their life.

Wart viruses are spread from other people's warts. When someone with plantar warts on their feet goes barefoot, they leave a trail of wart viruses behind them. This happens because the dead cells that make up the skin's keratin layer rub off when a person walks on a rough surface. The wart viruses that have pushed through the epidermis and into the keratin layer rub off too. If you walk barefoot in the same area, you may end up with some wart viruses on your skin.

About one in every eight children has warts. Do you think any of these children have warts?

Activity 2:
Seeing Is Believing

This activity shows how you can "catch" a plantar wart at a swimming pool. You will need a piece of sandpaper, two small potatoes, and a pepper shaker. Pretend that the sandpaper is the rough, nonslip floor surface around a pool, the potatoes are feet, and the pepper grains are wart viruses.

Rinse one potato under a stream of water and shake pepper on one side. Next, rub the pepper-covered side of the potato (the warty foot) across the sandpaper (the floor). Did some pepper-viruses get on the sandpaper?

Now wet the other potato. This potato represents your foot. Rub your potato-foot across the peppery sandpaper (the virus-covered floor). Did the sandpaper scrape through the potato's skin? If so, did some pepper get inside? Now you know how wart viruses get into your epidermis.

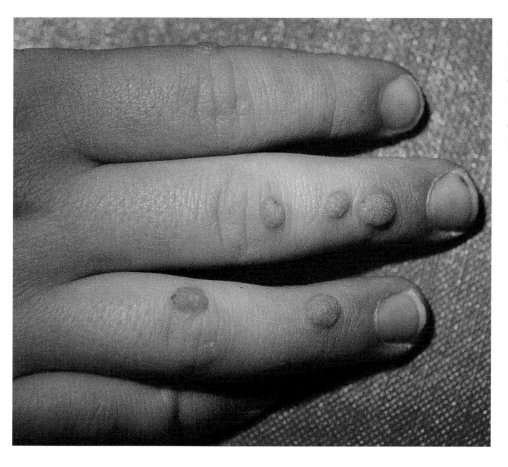

If this person throws a baseball, some wart viruses might tag along for the ride.

When someone with warty hands throws you a baseball, some of the wart viruses in his or her skin cells will probably rub off on the ball. When you catch the ball, some of the viruses will get on the skin of your hands.

The viruses that you pick up from other people are dormant. And remember, most dormant viruses can't cause trouble unless they get into living skin cells. But if you have a crack, a scrape, or a cut in your skin, the dormant viruses can get down into your epidermis. If they do, you might get a wart.

Here are some ways to avoid getting warts:
- Bare feet beware! Wear socks, sandals, or flip-flops where people go barefoot. That way it's harder to pick up someone's wart viruses.
- Don't use another person's towel or wear someone else's unwashed clothes. Wart viruses could be waiting for you!

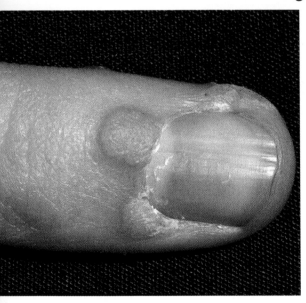

- Don't pick your hangnails. Wart viruses can get into those raw places.
- Always wash and bandage cuts so that viruses can't get into your skin.

If you have a wart, don't scratch it or rub it on other parts of your body. Your wart will spread viruses and can start new warts.

If you pick your hangnails, you might break open your skin. If you do, a papilloma virus can sneak in. A few months later, a wart may appear.

Mr. Papilloma W. Virus
32 Beach Hill Lane
Southampton, MA 01073

Papilloma W. Virus
32 Beach Hill Lane
Southampton, MA 01073

Dear Kids:

I'm in Massachusetts today, but I could be anywhere tomorrow. Some of my favorite places are locker rooms and shower floors. If you'd like to see me, remember not to wear flip-flops when you are there.

I also like people who wear dirty socks and don't wash their feet very often. If you share clothes with friends, bite your fingernails, pick your hangnails, or suck your thumb, we may be seeing each other soon. I look forward to that day.

Your friend,

Papilloma W. Virus

Getting Rid of Warts

It isn't easy to get rid of warts. But if you are patient, they will usually go away on their own. After a few weeks or a few months, most warts just disappear.

If you have embarrassing or painful warts that you can't stand, you might be able to get rid of them. People don't agree on the best way to get rid of warts. You could use over-the-counter medicines from a drugstore, **herbal medicines,** or even **folk remedies**—but you should probably begin by seeing a **dermatologist.**

A dermatologist is a doctor who treats skin diseases. The doctor might try to remove a wart using drops of acid or super-cold liquid nitrogen to freeze it. Sometimes, a dermatologist uses a laser beam to zap warts.

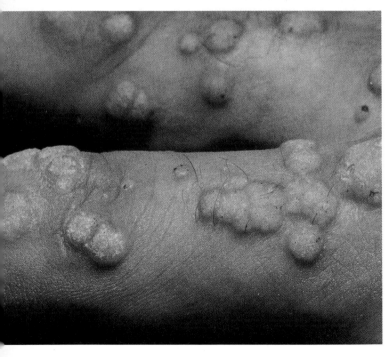

Believe it or not, these warts may just disappear.

If these methods don't work, the doctor might cut it out of your skin. The trouble with cutting out a wart is that it can leave a scar. And it still might not get rid of the wart. Warts can be tough!

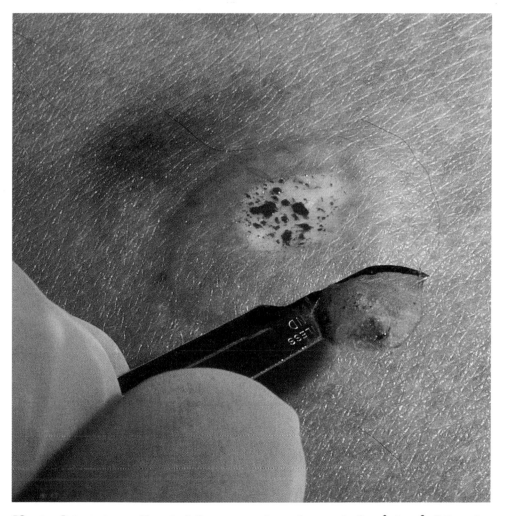

If you have a really stubborn wart, a dermatologist might cut it out of your skin.

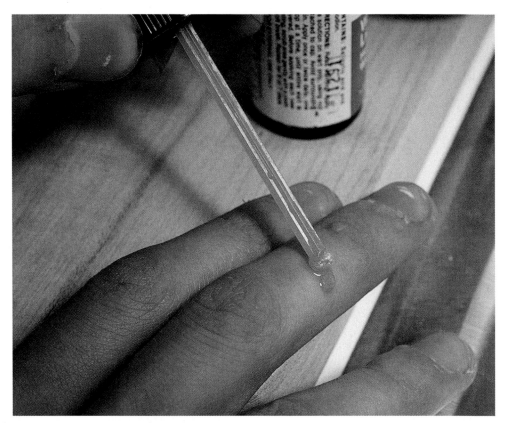

Drugstores sell wart treatments that you can use at home.

Most drugstores sell over-the-counter wart medicines that can be used at home. **Before using one of these medications, be sure to check with an adult. It is also important to read and follow the instructions on the package.** These medications are usually mild acids that you put right on the wart. When these medicines work, it usually takes 6 to 12 weeks to get rid of the wart completely.

Some people treat their warts with herbal medicines. These medicines are usually made from seeds, barks, roots, or flowers. Many of these treatments were developed by Native Americans or other native peoples who spent their lives learning about the chemicals in plants. The Chinese have hundreds of herbal remedies for diseases—including warts!

Herbal medicines used to fight warts include the sticky juices of dandelions, wintergreen oil, garlic, and the bark of the buckthorn tree. Sometimes Chinese healers place a slice of ginger root on top of a wart and cover it with burning mugwort. The burning plant helps the ginger produce chemicals that kill the virus.

For thousands of years, people have used folk remedies to try to get rid of warts. They have also tried to use charms, curses, hexes, and spells. There is no medical reason these "magical cures" should work, but some people still believe in them.

Herbs can be used to treat warts and many other illnesses.

Just for Fun

Before people knew what causes warts, they had all kinds of strange ideas about how to get rid of them.

- Place a silver bowl in the moonlight, wash your warty hands in the bowl, and say, "I wash my hands in thy dish; O man in the Moon, do grant my wish; And come and take away this."

- Take a hair from the tail of a white horse and tie it around the wart. Do not remove the hair until the wart falls off.

- Rub a bean pod over the wart, leave the pod by an ash tree, and say, "As this bean shell rots away; So my wart will soon decay."

- Flush a small twig of elderberry down the toilet and say, "Wart, wart, on my knee; please go, one, two, three."

- Cut off the head of an eel and drip the blood on your warts. Then bury the eel's head deep in the dirt. As the head rots, the warts will disappear.

- Rub your warts with a black snail. Rub nine times in one direction, and then nine times in the other direction. Stick the snail on a blackthorn bush. The warts will begin to die as the snail rots.

Preventing Warts

Why do some people get warts more often than others? Doctors and scientists think a person's health might have something to do with it. Your body has many defenses against viruses and other germs. It has a whole army of soldiers that fight for you—your **white blood cells.** They are part of your **immune system.**

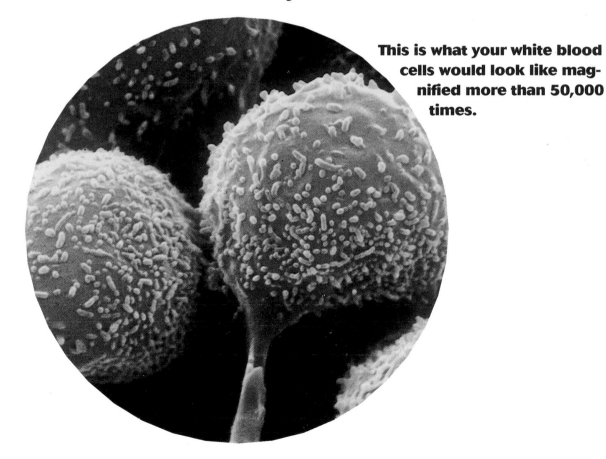

This is what your white blood cells would look like magnified more than 50,000 times.

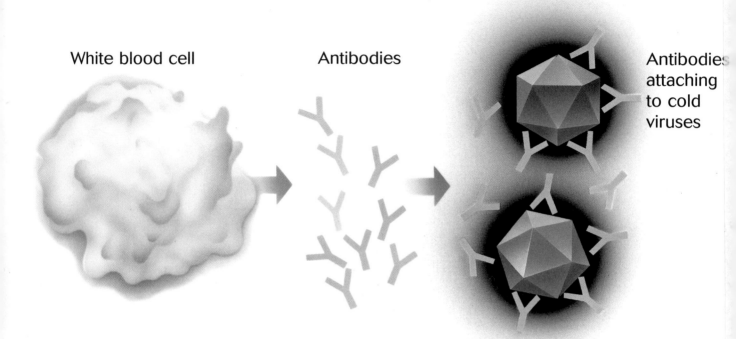

White blood cell

Antibodies

Antibodies attaching to cold viruses

When germs, such as these cold viruses, invade your body, some white blood cells produce antibodies. The antibodies attach to the germ and help destroy it.

Some white blood cells act like guards on patrol. They are always on the lookout for invaders. When they spot a virus, they send out chemical signals to call in other white blood cells to fight the germs. Some of them go after the germs and gobble them up. Others make proteins called **antibodies,** which are like ammunition for the white blood cell soldiers.

Antibodies may damage germs, or they may make it easier for the white blood cells to catch and kill the invaders.

After the battle is over, some of the antibodies stay in the body. If the same kind of virus invades again, those antibodies will recognize it and make a whole new supply of ammunition to fight the germs.

A healthy person has a stronger immune system than a sick person, so he or she can fight off germs more easily. When your immune system gets run down or weak, it has trouble fighting germs. That's why a healthy person may be less likely to get warts.

Eating healthful foods will help keep your immune system strong.

Getting plenty of exercise is a good way to stay healthy.

The best way to keep your immune system strong is to stay healthy. You can do this by eating well, exercising regularly, getting enough rest, and practicing clean habits (washing your hands and keeping your body, clothes, food, and dishes clean). If you can keep yourself healthy and strong, then your body's defenses will be strong enough to fight off invading viruses—including wart viruses.

Glossary

antibody—a protein produced by white blood cells; some antibodies help to kill germs

bacterium (plural **bacteria**)—a microscopic single-celled organism; some bacteria can cause illness

callus—skin that has been hardened by work or wear. Calluses usually appear on hands or feet.

capillaries—tiny blood vessels that look like black specks in warts

colony—a group of living things that live together

common wart—a pea-sized wart that has a rough, bumpy surface and usually appears on a person's face or hands

contagious—spread from one person to another

corn—a hard, painful growth of skin on toes

dermatologist—a doctor who treats skin problems, such as warts

dermis—the inner layer of living skin cells, beneath the epidermis. This layer also contains nerves and blood vessels

41

dormant—not active. Wart viruses are dormant outside of skin cells.

electron microscope—a powerful microscope needed to see viruses

epidermis—the outer layer of living skin cells

flat wart—a smooth wart that often grows in large groups on a person's face, arms, or back

folk remedy—using magic to try to cure an illness, such as warts

gland—an organ or group of cells that produces a substance that does some job in the body or passes out of the body

hair follicle—the tubelike structure in the skin from which a hair grows

herbal medicine—a natural medicine made from plant parts

immune system—the body's disease-fighting system, including white blood cells

keratin layer—the tough outer layer of skin that is made of dead cells

papilloma virus—the virus that causes warts in humans

plantar wart—a painful wart that grows on the soles of feet and on the toes

protein—a substance found in all plant and animal cells. Some proteins help support cells, while others speed up chemical reactions.

receptor—the "lock" on the outside of a cell. Wart viruses have proteins that fit the receptors on skins cells.

virus—a very tiny living thing that uses cells of other living things to reproduce

wart—a tough growth on the skin made by wart viruses

white blood cell—a blood cell that is an important part of the body's defenses. Some white blood cells eat germs and clean up bits of damaged cells and dirt.

Learning More

Books

Facklam, Howard and Margery. *Viruses*. New York: Twenty-First Century Books, 1994.

Shreve, Susan. *Warts*. New York: Tambourine Books, 1996.

Videos

The Immune System: Our Internal Defender. Shawnee Mission, Kansas: Marsh Film Enterprises, 1991.

Organizations and Online Sites

American Academy of Dermatology
930 N. Meacham Road
Schaumberg, IL 60173
http://www/aad.org

The Big Picture Book of Viruses

http://www.tulane.edu/~dmsander/Big_Virology/BVHomePage.html
This sounds like a little kid's picture book, but it is for teachers and students. It is full of amazing pictures of viruses taken with electron microscopes.

Cells Alive!

http://www.cellsalive.com
A great site for viewing pictures and computer "movies" of different kinds of cells.

KidsHealth.org

http://www.kidshealth.org

This site has loads of information on infections, behavior and emotions, food and fitness, and growing up healthy. It also has health games and animations. A search option lets you search for "warts" or other health conditions. The site was created and is maintained by medical experts at The Nemours Foundation.

Sympatico: HealthyWay: Health Links: Skin

http://www.sympatico.ca/healthyway/Directory

This is a Canadian site for parents and children. It provides information about all kinds of health conditions, including warts.

Index

Activities
  "catch" a wart, 29
  how small is a wart virus, 9
Animals and warts, *4*, 5, 12, *12*
Anthill, 8, *8*
Antibodies, 38–39, *39*

Black specks, 6–7, *24*, 26, *26*
Books, 44

Callus, *24*
Catching warts, 27–30, *27*, *29*, *30*
Children, 14, 20, 27, *27*
Colonies, 23
Color of warts, 5-6
Common warts, 20–21, *20*, *21*
Corns, 7, *7*
Cuts, 16–*17*, *17*, 29
Cutting warts out, 32-33, *33*

Dermatologist, 32–33

Exercise, 40, *40*

Faces, 20, 21, 24–26, *25*
Feet, *6*, *22*, 23, *24*, 27, 30
Fingers, 21, *29*, *30*
Flat warts, 24–26, *25*
Flu virus, 10, *10*
Folk remedies, 7, 32, 35–36
Freezing warts, 32
Frogs and toads, 5

Hair follicles, 14, *15*
Hands, 20, 21, 24, 29, *29*, 40
Hangnails, 30, *30*
Herbal medicines, 32, 35, *35*

Immune system, 37–40, *37*, *38*, *39*, *40*

Keiko, killer whale, *4*, 5

Medicines, 32, 34–35, *34*, *35*

Pain, 21, *22*, 23
Papilloma virus, 11–12, *11*, *19*
  catching, 27–31, *27*, *29*, *30*

size of, 9
where it lives, 12, 14, 16–18
Plantar wart, *22*, 23, *24*, 27–28
Polio virus, 10, *10*
Preventing warts, 37–40, *37,
38, 39, 40*

Scratching, 30
Sea turtle, *12*
Skin, 12, 13–18, *13*, *15*, *17*
life span of skin cell, 13
spreading warts, 27–30, *29,
30*

Toes, *23*, 24
Treatment
cutting warts out, 32-33, *33*
folk remedies, 7, 32, 35–36
freezing warts, 32
herbal medicines, 32, 35, *35*
over-the-counter, 32, 34, *34*
Twain, Mark, 7

Videos, 44
Viruses, 9–10, *10*, 13
defenses against, 37–40, *37,
38, 39, 40*
dormant virus, 11, 16, 29–30
wart virus. *See* Papilloma virus

Warts. *See also* Treatment
appearance, 5–7, *6*
avoiding warts, 30
catching, 27–30, *27, 29, 30*
cause of warts, 8–12, *11*
common warts, 20–21, *20,
21*
flat warts, 24–26, *25*
how long they last, 32
length of time to develop, 18
plantar warts, *22*, 23, *24*, 27
preventing, 37–40, *37, 38,
39, 40*
who gets warts, 14
White blood cell, 37–38, *37, 38*

About the Author

Michael P. Kinch is a professor and science librarian in Corvallis, Oregon. He has an undergraduate degree in biology, a master's degree in library science, and a master's degree in history of science. In his free time, Mr. Kinch enjoys camping, hiking, chasing lizards, and watching too many movies with his wife, Marjorie, and his two daughters, Ginger and Cindy. Mr. Kinch thinks warts are very interesting, but he really doesn't want any!